VISIONS TOWARDS UNITY

Published by Skylark,
191, Ringinglow Road,
Sheffield
S11 7PT
     www.Skylark-KL.co.uk

I.S.B.N. 0-9550735-0-2

© Kathryn Lausevic 2005

Printed by the Print & Design Shop,
279, Sharrow Vale Road, Sheffield, S11 8ZF

VISIONS TOWARDS UNITY

Guided Visualisations for Groups and Individuals,

Quotations and Illustrated Poems.

By Kathryn Lausevic

Dedicated to all the Spiritual Teachers and wonderful people who have inspired me with their wisdom, courage, humour and compassion.

Acknowledgements

My thanks go to David Cousins for the use of "Making the Body Transparent" and "Cleansing and Rebirth."

Many thanks to Lisa Davis for "The Crystal", adapted from her book, "Journeys Within," published by Findhorn Press.

I am grateful to Jean Bond for permission to use the quotation from her book, "Behind the Masks," published by Gateway Books.

Extracts from "The Tenth Insight" by James Redfield published by Bantam Press. Used by permission of Transworld Publishers, a division of The Random House Group Limited.

Many thanks to the White Eagle Publishing Trust for the use of two quotations from White Eagle magazines and one from "The Quiet Mind".

Grateful thanks to Sheila Sherwell for her help in writing down the music.

Thanks to John Wragg for proof-reading the book.

My heartfelt thanks go to my friend Ray, who helped me publish the book.

Finally I should like to thank all the people (incarnate or discarnate) whose wise words I have quoted;   If I have used a quotation without permission it means I have been unable to discover the source.

CONTENTS

VISUALISATIONS SPECIFICALLY FOR HEALING

POEMS AND SONGS

INTRODUCTION

Everything that is made begins with a thought. Every object, every task we perform, works of art and creative actions of all kinds, the styles of your clothes and designs of all descriptions including machines - all begin with an idea in someone's mind. Even the wheel was an idea in someone's mind, in prehistoric times, and what an invention! The power of the mind is unlimited - we can bring into reality whatever we focus on.

A thought can be positive or negative, or just a neutral thought. If we think positive thoughts we develop states of hope, acceptance, peace, joy and well-being, which incidentally contribute to a state of bodily good health. When we are feeling harmonious and at peace with ourselves, certain hormones are released which are beneficial to our bodies, enhancing the activity of the immune system. Conversely if we think negative thoughts, we develop habits of anxiety, suspicion, fear, anger, judgment, which can lead to stress in the body, the precursor to depression and illness.

Whatever we focus on increases our energy or detracts from it. This includes what we see on television, characters in books we are reading, what we read in the newspapers and so on. We receive positive energy from things we enjoy - whether it be music, poems, walking in the woods or whatever. This applies also to people we think about. If we let our thoughts dwell on those we have a "problem" with we will find that our energy decreases. Whereas if we turn our thoughts to those we love and feel happy with, our energy levels will rise.

Words are enormously powerful. Repetition of mantras, prayers, or even just certain words endows them with power. This power is then mirrored to us and enhances our energy. So words are tremendously important! And they have power to influence people - encouraging them, making them happy, or perhaps making them sad, even sometimes hurting them thoughtlessly. So we need always to be aware of what we say, how we say it and to whom.

"We cannot too strongly emphasise the power of thought... your thoughts are helping the world to enlightenment, or are holding back the progress of humanity... The power of thought must be guided by two cosmic principles - love and wisdom... Your thoughts are drawn through magnetic vibration towards other great thought streams, positive or negative. All positive thought - by this we mean thoughts that are good, uplifting, constructive - go forth from you, and by the law of attraction find great streams of thought which are positive, which are good, which belong to the Light."

White Eagle, from published teachings.

Creative visualisation is a form of meditation with thought. Like other methods of meditation, it involves stillness and concentration. Although we are receptive and relaxed during visualisation, thoughts and ideas come to us, often inspiring and empowering, enabling us to cause specific happenings to manifest, to come into being. Indeed, we are frequently motivated to act on information and inspirations which arise during the experience.

Because it can indirectly make things happen, visualisation brings responsibility. It must only be used for the highest purposes, for the common good. It must never be used to harm anyone.

Through practising visualisation we have the power to bring about change. We can instigate change in ourselves, even profound change - this is wonderful and amazing enough, but, of a greater magnitude, we can bring about changes to the planet. As Bearers of Light we can be instrumental in helping to heal the Earth. What a wonderful opportunity we have!

The benefits of this practice are many. First of all, visualisation can enable the heart centre to open to positive and creative energy, which in turn can be radiated to wherever or whoever you focus on. Secondly, because it turns the attention inward, it has the effect of stilling and relaxing the busy mind and body. This relaxed state can bring wisdom as well as knowledge, for regular practice awakens and increases psychic abilities. Furthermore it brings clarity and understanding, which can have a beneficial effect on relationships and everyday life.

"When the minds of the group are in harmony, when they are open and intuitive, when they are attuned to the Godhead, then cosmic energy flows down to permit those minds to create on a level hitherto impossible."
From "The Wisdom of Ramala," channelled to the Ramala Centre, Glastonbury.

It has been proved that the collective power of a group is greater than that generated by the sum of the individuals.

Although the visualisations in this book have been used mainly for groups, there is no reason why you should not use them as and when you need to, on an individual basis, especially the ones for healing. You may find them useful at different times, according to your need of the moment.

The more relaxed you are, the better they will work. One way to use them is to record them, either yourself, or ask someone you know whose voice you like. At first, when reading them, it is a common error to read too quickly - you will have to experiment with this, to get the pace and pauses that suit you best. You may wish to play relaxing background music, which enhances the experience for some people - it is your choice.

If you don't want to fall asleep during the visualisation it may be best to assume a sitting posture, but make sure that the head, neck and spine are aligned; this is really important as it allows the energy to flow through your body.

The place you choose should preferably be the same each time, somewhere you feel comfortable and safe, a place where you won't be disturbed. You may like to unplug the phone for greater peace and relaxation.

To prepare yourself for the visualisation, practise breathing slowly and deeply. This allows the mind and body to slow down and helps to turn the awareness inwards.

All of the visualisations in the book are tried and tested - they have been used with groups for a number of years. Now it is time to share them with others, but please do not feel they should be used rigidly - word for word. They are meant to be a basis for creative ideas of your own, and can of course, be adapted accordingly. They are dynamic in that they can be altered to suit the need. Please change them as you like, in order to keep them fresh and flowing.

The poems are ones which came to me usually while walking, or sometimes in meditation. I have included mainly recent ones, as they seem to express how I am now. I do not profess to be a poet; they just express feelings and thoughts of the moment when they arose.

The quotations are ones which have inspired me personally, ones which I have thought worth sharing; some of them are about planetary awareness.

As well as preparation for visualisation I have included some ways of "grounding" after meditation or visualisation, as some people may feel out of touch with their surroundings for a while afterwards.

The book is meant to be enjoyed - so I sincerely hope you will use it and enjoy it!

"We are all souls in growth; we all have an original intention that is positive; and we can all remember. Our responsibility is to hold that idea for everyone we meet. That's the true interpersonal Ethic; that's how we uplift, that's the contagion of the new awareness that is encircling the planet."

James Redfield - The Tenth Insight.

Note:- If working with a group of mentally handicapped people, it is advisable to use very simple visualisations only, as the more complex ones, which involve "leaving your body" - i.e. visualising yourself in a different location - can lead to potential problems afterwards; some people may find it difficult to "come back" into their bodies, back to day-to-day reality. Ones which would be suitable would be to bring the light in and imagine small suns in the heart, head, hands and feet, then expand the light, etc. You can be quite creative with this!

Chelsea Park - Sunday - 8 a.m.

Grass: long, waving, fragrant.
Trees: strong, solid, verdant.
Clouds: fluffy, puffy, buoyant.

Flowers: varied, colourful, glowing.
Dog: barking; cock: crowing.
Sun: dappling, glimmering, shimmering.

Swings: empty, inviting, delighting.
Birds: feeding, trilling, winging.
Me: blissful, singing, swinging.

5

THE AURA AND THE CHAKRAS

The aura is a basic concept of ancient Eastern traditions, which is now commonly accepted in the West. In addition to our physical body we have an energy body; this surrounds all living things. This was not proven until the twentieth century, although many psychics were able to see it and interpret it. A doctor, Dr. Kilner, discovered a way of seeing the aura by using a special screen. He was able to diagnose illnesses from studying auras, but his findings were dismissed by the medical establishment.

Nowadays Kirlian photography is often used to photograph the aura.

The aura consists of coloured light, which extends around the body, usually about four to six inches beyond the physical body. It varies according to the energy level of the person, to their emotional, physical, mental and spiritual state. The colours of the aura are determined by the chakras, the seven main energy centres of the body. There are many energy centres, as an acupuncturist will tell you, but the ones we are concerned with here are the seven main ones, which are situated along the spine. These areas receive cosmic vibrations and put them into circulation. This circulatory energy is the Kundalini, which is represented by a flow of pure white light which is able to balance our physical and spiritual body.

People who can see chakras say they look like pulsating wheels which rotate rhythmically from the centre outwards, as though spilling out from the centre. Any changes in the vibration will change the energy which physiologically can cause disease to develop. These changes are shown in the altered colour of the chakra. If there is an imbalance on a chakra it can look dirty. Sometimes there is a block, caused by unused energy, or the chakra energy is too strong and again causes an imbalance. Both of these states can lead to malfunction and illness. But when the chakras are all evenly balanced and harmonised, the mind, body, and spirit will work in perfect harmony. There are various ways of dealing with an imbalance, which I won't go into here, but meditation and/or visualisation is one way to redress any imbalances in the chakras.

The colours of the chakras are seen only with the "inner eye" - some people can see them easily but most find they receive more a "sense" of the colour - this ability can be developed with practice. The colours are usually considered to be the ones seen in a rainbow - the whole spectrum in fact. There are musical notes connected with them too - and interestingly, there are seven "main" notes (without sharps or flats) in the western scale - as there are seven predominant colours in the rainbow.

Each chakra reflects a different quality. Someone who is especially psychic or sensitive, who is not interested in the physical life is usually based in the higher chakras, while a person who is interested in sport, say, but not very aware of the spiritual or psychic side of his nature is probably centred more in his lower chakras. Both of these people may be "out of balance".

The Base Chakra

Located in the genital area, facing downwards to earth, it is connected with the Earth, survival, the release of emotional tension and aggression. The qualities associated with it include the Earth qualities of stability, practicality, courage, determination, decisiveness. On a physical level it is connected with the large intestine, the lower part of the pelvis, the hips, legs and feet. It is linked to the endocrine system through the adrenal glands.

If the root chakra is out of balance, we may have a feeling of unreality, of being "spaced out". This can lead to accident proneness. It is important to balance the root chakra, as this "grounds" us, keeping us connected to the present and to the everyday world. Imbalances on a physical level include constipation, obesity, poor circulation in legs and feet, arthritis and knee problems.

When in balance it vibrates to a clear red.

The Sacral Chakra

This is the second chakra in the chakra system, located about three fingers below the navel. It is connected with creativity and sexuality and the joy of the inner child. Physically linked with the sacral centre are the reproductive organs, the kidneys, bladder, the lower digestive organs and the lower back.

Imbalances can lead to depression, hysteria, and a weak personality. Physically it is connected to lower back trouble, pre-menstrual and reproductive problems and urinary problems.

Any work done to balance the sacral centre will have a corresponding effect on the physical circumstances and condition. If you have problems or traumas with the sexual side of your life, especially difficulties which stem from childhood experiences, work on the sacral centre will help to heal old wounds. The sacral centre is also connected with emotions in that it enables us to sense other people's emotions and feelings and to empathise with them; also it develops an awareness of possibly dangerous or emotionally-charged situations and atmospheres. For instance when entering a room we can sometimes "pick up" unpleasant or inharmonious vibrations which reflect something that has taken place there. By the same token, we can sense a peaceful, harmonious atmosphere, room or house.

Sometimes we "take on" other people's emotions and feelings, especially if the chakra is wide open. If it is wide open you may feel:

- drained by contact with other people,
- emotionally charged by other people's problems, even though they are nothing to do with you,
- constantly aware of "atmospheres" and tensions which other people seem unaware of.

Anyone who works with other people, e.g. teachers, nurses, therapists, social workers, etc., should pay special attention to the sacral chakra, as it can help to protect against becoming disturbed by others' emotions and problems.

The colour is orange.

The Solar Plexus Chakra

This is situated above the navel, in the place where we feel "butterflies in the stomach." It has to do with feelings, the intellect and also the digestion. The emotions, food and the mind are closely connected and the solar plexus is where the "lower" emotions are based - anger, anxiety, resentment, jealousy, insecurity and so on - all the feelings connected with fear. Each chakra affects the one next to it, so if the chakra below, i.e. the sacral chakra is not functioning properly, the digestion can be affected.

Linked with the solar plexus chakra are the pancreas, spleen, stomach, liver, gall bladder and middle back.

Imbalances in the solar plexus centre can lead to addictive and compulsive behavior, sleep problems, and excessive anger or fear. Physically it may lead to stomach problems, diabetes, allergies, anorexia and obesity.

Work on the solar plexus leads to a feeling of being empowered and in control. It also improves mental clarity.

When in balance, the colour is a bright, clear yellow. If this is a very strong buttercup yellow, it indicates an academic person who is very much involved with his own interests.

The Heart Chakra

This is located in the centre of the chest. It is the place of the soul, of inner guidance, of the higher emotions such as unconditional love and all feelings connected with it - compassion, empathy, friendship and understanding.

At a physical level, the associated organs include the heart and lungs, and the immune system; it is also connected with the circulatory system, bronchial tubes, chest, arms and upper back. The associated gland is the thymus gland.

Imbalances are associated with inner conflict, self-destructive tendencies, problems with relationships and feelings of isolation. On a physical level it is associated with circulatory and respiratory problems and problems with the upper back.

When in balance, the colour is a clear grass green.

The Throat Chakra

This is associated with all forms of communication and self-expression - speaking, singing, dancing, music - both performing and listening, and other forms of creativity, expression and communication. On a subtle level, it is to do with truth, peace and order, giving and receiving.

Physically the throat chakra is linked to the pharynx, neck and throat, the lymphatic and neurological systems. Being connected to the mouth and teeth, ears and nose, it is also linked with the senses of hearing, tasting and smelling.

Imbalances in the chakra can lead to a difficulty in expressing oneself and doubting the sincerity of others. Physical imbalances are linked with sore throats, teeth, ear, neck and shoulder problems, bronchitis and hearing and speech problems.

It is connected with the thymus, thyroid and parathyroid glands.

The colour when in balance is a sky blue or turquoise.

The Third Eye (Brow Chakra)

This is located in the middle of the forehead, inside the skull. As well as balancing the power of the mind and logical thinking and reasoning, it is connected with clarity and insight and an interest in spirituality. Being the place of intuition, spiritual perception and the mystical and psychic life, it allows soul knowledge to develop and can bring feelings of ecstasy.

Imbalances on this chakra can lead to confusion, poor memory, an inability to focus and a feeling of detachment from reality. Physically it is linked with nervous upsets, problems with vision, headaches and sinusitis.

The brow chakra is linked with the brain, eyes and face, also the nerves of the head. The associated glands are the pituitary and the hypothalamus.

The colour is indigo.

The Crown Chakra

This is situated on top of the head. It is where spiritual energies can enter, dealing with all spiritual issues. It provides a direct link with the Source and is connected with goodness, beauty and artistic qualities, also with intuition and higher realms. It develops experience of direct knowing and integration of the personality with the Spirit.

At a physical level it connects with the right brain hemisphere and the rest of the body. Imbalances can cause nightmares, multiple personalities and being spiritually closed; physically it is linked to migraine headaches, pituitary problems and epilepsy.

The pineal is the associated gland.

The colour is violet.

"Be the change you want to see in the world." - Mahatma Gandhi.

THE CHAKRA SYSTEM

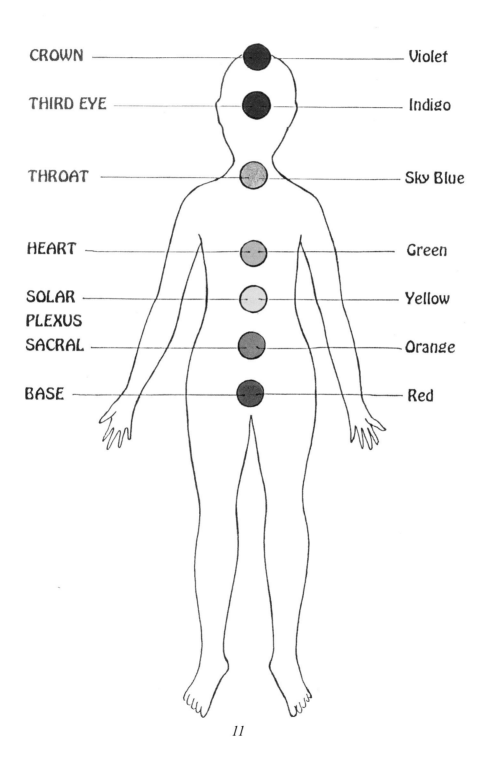

CROWN —————————— Violet

THIRD EYE —————————— Indigo

THROAT —————————— Sky Blue

HEART —————————— Green

SOLAR —————————— Yellow
PLEXUS

SACRAL —————————— Orange

BASE —————————— Red

Harmony

If I am in harmony
        With myself
        With my family
        With my friends
        With my world,
So will my body be.
And a beautiful Healing
Will take place in me.

PREPARATION FOR VISUALISATION

Sit comfortably on your seat, relaxed, but with the spine straight. Now imagine a thread from the crown chakra (top of the head), linking you to the ceiling. Just welcome yourself to this time of relaxation and stillness - a special time just for you.

Be aware of how you are sitting. Sitting with the head, neck and spine in alignment allows the energy to vibrate through your body. The feet should be firmly on the floor, and the hands should be resting comfortably in your lap. Slow the breathing down - breathe gently and steadily. As you breathe out, feel the tension leaving your body. (Expand this if required.) Be aware of your body; if any part of you feels tense, just move it slightly until it is comfortable. Next time you breathe out, let go of any thoughts, ideas or opinions... just let them float away into the air... until you feel quite empty... (Pause.)

Just have the feeling that you are here to relax, letting go of everything... nowhere to go, nothing to do but sit here and relax... letting go... letting go...

GROUNDING

At the end of meditation or visualisation, it is important to make sure that you get back to a state of normality - of being in the present moment - aware of being in touch with everything around you, in other words, not to be "spaced out!"

Ways of doing this include:-

1) Imagine that your hands and feet are magnets. Take a deep breath and let it out all in one go. At the same time, bring your astral body down into your physical body.

2) Sniff air in seven times; imagine a spiral round your body, spiralling upwards as you breathe in. When the lungs are full, "whoosh" the air out all in one go.

3) Imagine a cord from the base of your spine going down into the earth. Sit still for a few moments, feeling connected.

4) Stamp on the floor for a few seconds, alternate feet, at the same time breathing deeply.

"Time is what keeps the light from reaching us. There is no greater obstacle to God than time. "

Meister Eckhart.

Peak Experience

Into the cupboard with the sliding door
Behind the settee - time, about seven-
Onto a groaning shelf I stuffed
My homework file; I was eleven.

My father sat, the radio on -
Deep in the armchair (leather, worn),
Relaxing, still, weary from work;
Occasionally he gave a yawn.

All of a sudden I stood, stock still,
As if a lightning bolt had struck my head;
A unique moment, never lost -
"What is this music, Dad?" I said.

He told me what the music was -
"Polovtsian Dances, Prince Igor."
The angel voices rang out true;
I heard the heavenly sound with awe.

That life was precious, full of joy
My mind was clear as morning air;
And I would never be the same
As once I was - I was aware.

BRINGING ELEMENTAL QUALITIES TO OURSELVES

Preparation for visualisation.

Now in your mind's eye, see yourself out in the countryside, walking in a rather wild area, in a beautiful valley, with a river running through. You are walking along a path near the river... there are gorse bushes and many wild flowers and lush vegetation. The sun is shining and you can feel its warmth. You are following the path carefully, as it leads gently upwards... (pause.)

The air is fresh and you start to breathe deeply, filling your lungs with its wonderful life-giving properties. So as you walk along, you begin to fill yourself with these qualities. The properties of the air element include:- lightness, joyfulness, clarity, inspiration, spontaneity, humour, creativity and the ability to communicate.

Clarity is the ability to see through appearances to the reality, the essence of things. The air element gives us the ability to see joy and opportunity in all the challenges which life presents us with. Also it contains an almost childlike quality of trust, with wonder, excitement, expectancy and a playful, lighthearted attitude. So as I repeat these qualities, you might like to breathe them into your body, and as you breathe out let them settle in the core of your being, to become part of you. (Repeat list of qualities with pauses.)

In American Indian tradition, the Spirit of Air is symbolised by the eagle, which can soar higher than any other bird and represents heightened perception, the eye that encompasses all possibilities.

So as you walk along the little path, you feel joyful, light-hearted and full of expectancy and confidence... (Pause.)

You can hear the water gurgling and splashing and gradually the sound becomes louder - more of a rushing sound. As you walk round a bend in the path you see before you a waterfall - a beautiful, sparkling cascade of water tumbling over the rocks... you pause to look at it, then notice that there is a narrow path which leads to a spot, a sort of shelf, actually below the waterfall... you are feeling rather hot by now, with the heat of the sun and the exercise... so you decide to strip off your clothes and go to stand beneath the tumbling water. Treading very gingerly you make your way along the narrow path until you reach this shelf, where the water is splashing and frothing... you step into the waterfall and can see the clear droplets of water glistening and shining in the sun... each one is like a tiny, clear crystal. You feel the coolness of the water as it falls on you... it seems to cleanse your body right through... it is washing away all tension, fear, pain, resentment or any other negative feelings you may be carrying around with you... (Pause.) All these negative tendencies are washed down out of your body, out through the arms, hands and fingers, then down through the legs, feet and toes. As it does this, it replaces these feelings with its own elemental qualities. The properties of water include:- intuition, flexibility, gentleness together with strength, humility, receptivity and an ability to flow with everything. It enables you to know your own worth and to make decisions from a place of knowingness within. Water is humble because it always finds the lowest level. Water represents the qualities most associated with women - nurturing, caring and feeling with an ability to listen to others and empathise with them. This takes skill, patience and a willingness to be open, flexible and vulnerable. So as I repeat these qualities, imagine them washing down through you... (Repeat list with pauses.)

Now it is time to leave the water, so you step out of the waterfall and make your way back to where you have left your clothes. By this time you are practically dry with the heat of the sun, and after dressing yourself you decide to have a rest, lying on some soft grass in the sunshine...

So as you lie down comfortably, you can feel the sun's rays filling your body, making you feel very relaxed... (Pause.)

The sunshine brings us the fire element and this begins to fill your body with its powerful attributes.

The fire qualities include:- courage, energy, enthusiasm and creativity.

The fire element is the power to take action, to be decisive and to be able to say "No", when appropriate, as well as saying "Yes" to one's true feelings, to new opportunities and to Life! Many women, and men too have been programmed or trained to give their power away to others... we have to learn the creative magic of saying "Yes" or "No". The energy of fire is released through the decision to act. Once we know in our hearts the right thing to do and act on it, energy comes to our aid. Energy follows thought and action!

So, as I repeat these qualities, you might like to breathe them in and feel they are a part of you. (Repeat list with pauses.)

Lying on the grass we make contact with the Earth...

Feel the strength, the stability of the Earth, supporting you.

So finally we are going to bring the Earth qualities to ourselves. These include:- practicality, determination, logical thinking, strength and stability, patience, and being centred or grounded.

Strength enables us to follow our true spiritual nature and purpose. As I repeat the qualities, breathe them in and feel them become established in your body, until they become a part of you. (Repeat list with pauses.)

So feel the solidity and strength of the earth supporting you, filling you with energy, grounding you until you feel at one with the Earth... you feel a unity and harmony with everything that is - with the Earth, the air, the water, the sun, the sky, the trees and all living things.(Pause.)

Now gradually become aware of this room, etc.

"You are a child of the elements, composed of and part of the elements.
How can you possibly think you are separate?
How can you possibly not know that when the wind blows it is part of you,
that the sun gives to you and is part of you with each sunbeam,
that from the water you came and the water joins you all,
that without the air you breathe you could not live?
How can you not know that if one suffers,
the whole consciousness of the Earth partakes of that?
When one rejoices,
the whole consciousness knows and is part?"

Lord of the Elements.

September

In Whiteley Woods
All is still.
The far trees -
Ghosts in the mist -
Some like soldiers,
Tall and straight,
Some, old men,
Frail and bent;
Another, horizontal -
An insect-haven.

Sitting on a crocodile log,
Under the turning birches,
I hear the bird chorus.
What is their song -
A random sound, or
Meaningful messages
Of Love, of Food, of Hope?
On this autumn morning
Their joyful chatter
Fills my heart with gladness.

VISUALISATION FOR THE NEW YEAR

Begin with preparation for meditation, as above.

Will you please imagine a white light above your head, coming down into your head through the crown chakra, down through the energy centres, filling the body. It permeates your whole body... going to every cell, soothing, relaxing and healing. It takes away all negativity... fear... anxiety... pain... leaving you completely relaxed. This is the Father energy from above. It brings love, compassion and wisdom. As you breathe in, imagine this light filling your whole body. On every outbreath become more and more relaxed. (Pause.)

Now in the centre of the earth there is white light, energy in the form of heat. In your mind's eye, imagine that your feet have roots which spread downwards into the earth. Now draw up the beautiful white energy from the earth... up through your roots into your feet... through your legs and into the lower chakras. It goes through the solar plexus and then into the heart centre. This is the Mother energy of the Earth. In the heart centre it meets the Father energy, producing an entity of love and compassion... a new YOU... you are like a butterfly emerging from a chrysalis... So with every breath, feel yourself more centred in the light... filled with love... universal, unconditional love and compassion for all beings. (Pause.)

Now imagine that you are standing in the countryside. In front of you is a little path which leads through a wooden gate to a hill beyond. It may be a place you are familiar with, or one which is created from your imagination.

In your mind's eye you walk along the little path to the gate, lift the latch, open the gate and go through... and then begin to follow the path up the hillside. Here and there are rocks and boulders... you can see the yellow gorse bushes and banks of purple heather... you feel the cool breeze against your face and smell the sweet scent of the wild flowers. Sometimes you pause to look at the view, then continue on your way.

Soon you reach the top. You are ready for a rest, so you choose a nearby boulder to sit on, from where you can see the view.

Now imagine that in one direction, the left, in your mind's eye you can see the year that has just passed. You might like to recall some of the events which took place in your life during this year. Whether you perceive them as "good" or "bad", remember that every experience has something to show us, something from which we have the opportunity to derive what we need for our growth... (Pause.)

Next, look at your achievements during the year - the projects you have completed successfully and anything you have learned during the year. Think especially about the last few months. Have you changed in any way during the year? Look at any hopes, dreams and ambitions you had - did you fulfil any of these? (Pause.)

Now look at yourself as you are in this moment in time. Are you any different from how you were a year ago?... Any changes for the better?... or worse?... Have you learned anything about yourself? (Pause.)

Remember that the real achievements are not the tasks we perform each day but are revealed in our attitudes to the problems which arise in our lives. It is not so much what we do but how we do it that is important... this is where the inner growth takes place.

Maybe there is something in your life or in yourself which you would like to change or even eliminate, so you may like to think of that for a moment. (Pause.)

Now in your mind's eye, turn to look in another direction - to the right. On this side we look into the future, into (name the year.)

Be aware of any feelings you may have about the coming year...

Are you looking forward to anything? (Pause.)

Are you afraid of anything? (Pause.)

Think about your hopes and dreams... what do you hope to achieve during the year? (Pause.)

If there is something you would like to change about yourself, what would it be? How would you begin to do that ? (Pause.)

Now, in your mind's eye, picture yourself as you would like to be in the coming year... imagine yourself doing the things you would like to do... being with the people you would like to be with, or, if you prefer, alone... see yourself in that situation... (Pause.)

Perhaps you would like to make some affirmations or resolutions for yourself. (Pause.)

So you are sitting on your boulder on the hilltop, and the sun is shining. You can feel the warmth of the sun's rays, filling your body with warmth and light. You are feeling very peaceful, with a strong sense of connectedness to everything around you... a sense of unity with all life... (Pause.)

Now we are going to radiate the light, which is the energy of love and compassion, to anyone who needs it. So each time you breathe in, fill yourself with more light, more energy. Then as you breathe out, focus on whoever you are sending it to, and see them shining in the light... complete, whole and perfect.

First you may like to send it to families and friends, and especially to anyone you know who is suffering in any way just now. (Pause.)

Now you might like to send it to anyone you have had a problem with in the past year, maybe someone you have hurt in some way, or who has hurt you. If so, you might like to make peace with them in your own way, maybe silently asking their forgiveness and surrounding them with light... (Pause.) ...and feel forgiveness in your own heart... this has a healing effect on yourself... (Pause.)

Now we are going to intensify the light so that it becomes a brilliant, white, shining field of energy...

Let us turn our attention to all people on this planet who are suffering in any way, perhaps through war or natural disasters, or for whatever reason. We send this loving energy to all lonely people, bereaved, sick people and anyone who needs it... Universal, unconditional love and compassion... (Pause.)

Next let us send it to all life on the earth - to all humanity, then to all the animals, the beings who share this remarkable planet with us... to the mammals... birds... fish... reptiles and insects... and especially to any creatures who suffer at the hands of man, such as ones kept in confined spaces, or ones who are cruelly treated... in our imagination, let us see them roaming free and undisturbed. (Pause.)

Then we send the light to the plant kingdom... to the trees, especially ones in danger of being cut down unnecessarily... then to the crops and food plants, and plants of all kinds... let us give thanks for their bountiful gifts to us. (Pause.)

Next we send the light to the mineral kingdom... the rocks, stones and crystals of the earth, and thank them for supplying essential minerals for our bodies. (Pause.)

Finally let us put our awareness in the planet herself, Mother Earth, who nurtures and sustains us. Let us silently give thanks to her for supplying all our needs. (Pause.)

The Earth is desperately in need of help at this present time, and dependent on our co-operation to help in the healing process. We are caretakers of the planet and as such, have the responsibility to live in harmony with her, and to learn not to take without giving back. In our mind's eye, let us now see all life on this planet living in harmony and unity with our mother, the Earth... Let us imagine the earth surrounded by beautiful white, shining light, suspended in space like a bauble on a Christmas tree. It looks so beautiful hanging there, turning slowly in the bright, shimmering light... it is a wonderful, precious, living being, the earth which is our home.

It is time now to leave the hilltop, so see yourself standing up and making the descent down the little path, which winds through the rocks and bushes, until you once more reach the gate at the bottom. Going through the gate you find yourself back where you started. (Pause.)

Now gradually return to this room... be aware of the texture of the chair you are sitting on, and the position you are sitting in.

You may be feeling in a vulnerable state, open to all kinds of influences, so before we open our eyes we are going to protect ourselves. This is a useful exercise to do any time you need psychic protection, for example from negative influences of any kind.

So, just to protect yourself, on the in-breath, once more breathe in a clear golden light. Feel it settle as you breathe out, making a bubble of light all around you. This allows positive vibrations into your aura but keeps out the negative ones. Repeat this twice more. (Pause.)

So now you are centred and protected, ready to begin the first day of the first week of the New Year. (Pause.)

I would like to make a suggestion. If there is anything you would like to change or eliminate in your life, you might like to write it on a piece of paper and either keep it to remind yourself, or throw it into a fire. This may be something like a bad habit you would like to get rid of, or perhaps some change in your life of some description.

Thank you for taking part in this visualisation.

"Change your thoughts if you wish to change your circumstances. Since you alone are responsible for your thoughts, only you can change them. You will want to change them when you realise that each thought creates according to its own nature."

Paramahansa Yogananda.

Women's Retreat Weekend

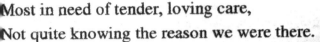

We came, like ships, into the harbour;
All ages, aspects, set on different courses -
Some wind-blown, weary, tossed by angry seas;
Some in full sail, assured, certain of their route,
Others burdened with heavy cargo, needing to release;
Most in need of tender, loving care,
Not quite knowing the reason we were there.

What did we find? A safe haven, place of peace,
A space to moor our temporary craft.
A chance to unravel the tangled ropes
Of life's vicissitudes; to find our souls once more.

Through loving, thoughtful care, sharing our needs
Our hopes, our fears, nurturing one another,
Some giving, some receiving - aren't they both the same?
We are refreshed, renewed. We claim our power,
Co-creators of our destiny; able to achieve!

We take on board just what we need
To meet the challenges we face,
And with replenished love and strength
Once more return to base.

SUMMER SOLSTICE

Let us ask our guides and angels to be with us this evening as we share the fun and joy in celebrating this, the longest day of the year.

On this solstice evening, let us invoke the Light to illuminate our minds, the Spirit of Love to enter our hearts, and the power of the Universal Spirit to guide and help us to bring about peace and healing in ourselves and our amazing planet, which is suffering so much as the result of Man's departure from Nature and harmony.

So we ask that Light , Love and Peace will descend on Earth.

(Songs or chants here if wished, e.g. The Great Invocation; Gayatri Mantra.)

As the sun goes down, we will chant the OM.

(Read from The Gospel of the Essenes - The Communions of the Ancient Wisdom - P.31-37.)
A Visualisation for the planet. (Suggestion: Floating in the Cosmos)

Chief Seattle said,"This we know. The Earth does not belong to Man; Man belongs to the Earth. This we know.
All things are connected like the blood which unites one family. All things are connected.
Whatever befalls the Earth befalls the sons of the Earth. Man did not weave the web of Life: he is merely a strand in it. Whatever he does to the web, he does to himself.
Even the white man, whose God walks and talks with him as friend to friend, cannot be exempt from the common destiny.
We may be brothers after all. We shall see."

Let us remember that we are brothers and sisters not only of everyone here, but of all people throughout the world and of all creatures, remembering to love and care for those who need our help or those who are weaker than ourselves, for as John Randolph Price says, "This is the beginning of Peace and Goodwill towards all, as Love flows forth from every soul, and all hearts and minds are in one perfect understanding."

PRAYER - hold hands in a circle.

O Great Spirit,   We are children of the Universe, all belonging to one great human family. Help us to raise our consciousness of You and all living things, and especially our Mother the Earth, so that we may live in peace and understanding, in brotherly helpfulness and co-operation. Through our actions, words and open hearts let us be instrumental in healing our planet.   Amen.

Now allow your awareness to rest on each person in the circle and radiate some love to each one, coming back to yourself. Don't forget to include yourself in this.

Let us silently thank the Universe for this opportunity of sharing we have had this evening. (Pause.) ...Thank you.

THE GREAT INVOCATION

From the point of Light within the Mind of God
Let light stream forth into the minds of men.
Let Light descend on Earth.

From the point of Love within the Heart of God
Let love stream forth into the hearts of men.
May Christ return to Earth.

From the centre where the Will of God is known
Let purpose guide the little wills of men -
The purpose which the Masters know and serve.

From the centre which we call the race of men
Let the Plan of Love and Light work out
And may it seal the door where evil dwells.

Let Light and Love and Power
restore the Plan on Earth.

Lightworker

Being an aerial,
Catching energy waves,
(Which, transformed
To Healing Light,
Compassionate Love,
Are then transmitted
To suffering souls,
To sacred Earth ,)
Completes a circuit
Within myself.

When people arrive, have numerous pieces of paper for them to write names of people, places, etc. who need healing. Place these on central table, (or floor) together with candles, incense, water, earth (plant or crystal), and anything they have brought. Suggest they may like to tell us about what they have brought and what it means to them.

Welcome.
Today thousands of people all over the earth are coming together to help to further the awakening of planetary consciousness and to hold a collective vision of Universal love and peace.
It has been proved that the collective meditation of a group is many times more powerful than the sum of individuals meditating. And today we join up with many people to do this work, all meditating at the same time. The crucial times are 5a.m., 1p.m. and 8 p.m. Greenwich Mean time. So at 8 p.m. we must make sure that we are doing the meditation, which should last at least 20 minutes.
We shall spend this evening focusing on the earth; we shall have a guided visualisation followed by a silence for meditating. Later on we may sing one or two songs and I have brought some quotations which I hope you will help me with.

This evening let us try to keep a vision of a world in which all live in peace, harmony and joy. See conflict resolved through Spirit, suffering lifted through compassion; and all darkness turning to light. You may feel a new awareness of our connection with one another... and sense the ripples of what we are doing spreading out to all.

But first let us start with a prayer.

O Great Spirit, Creator of the Universe, we have met with simplicity and love. We seek the place of purity, truth and wisdom within the centre of our Being, and call upon the angels of peace to bring us their wisdom and understanding, filling our hearts with their own compassion - towards ourselves and towards all living creatures and things.
We pray that there may radiate from this room a beautiful light and healing power to bring peace to men's hearts and to all living things. May this light spread throughout the world, as each of us plays a part in the great service of enlightenment, until the whole planet is a shining , shimmering globe of Light and Love. Amen.

We are going to sound the OM three times... you don't have to wait for the person next to you or sing the same note as them; we all have our own note... can we keep it continuous please, if possible. (Sound the OM).

Sit comfortable but relaxed etc. Take some deep breaths. On the inbreath , just feel

relaxed and peaceful. On the exhalation, let go of any thoughts, notions or worries you may
have... see them float away into the air. Feel very safe. Let the eyes and face become softer,
more peaceful, go yet more deeply into the softness and the peace. Allow yourself just to flow. (Pause.)

Your feet are planted firmly on the floor. Now in your imagination see yourself in a clearing in a wood, lying near a stream. The sun is shining, warming your whole body. You can hear the water gurgling nearby, and feel the freshness of the pure air that surrounds you. You feel at one with the elements - the air, with the qualities of lightness, spontaneity, clarity, lightness, light- heartedness and joy. As you breathe in, you feel these wonderful qualities entering your body. (Pause.)

Then as you lie in the sun you feel the power of the fire energy, and as you breathe in you fill yourself with these qualities - energy, enthusiasm, dynamism, creativity and courage, remembering that as we put our ideas into action, the energy always follows. (Pause.)

As we lie there we hear the bubbling of the stream nearby, and now we enter the sensation of the flowing water, become one with it. It brings to us the power to be receptive, flexible, intuitive and nurturing, to flow with everything. It gives us the ability to listen to others with an open, compassionate heart. (Pause.)

Finally, as we feel the softness of the ground we are lying on, we make contact with Mother Earth. The St. Francis prayer, "Lord, grant me the serenity to accept the things I cannot change, courage to change the things I can, and the wisdom to know the difference" evokes the spirit of the earth. This is shown in the qualities of determination, patience, practicality, stability and strength. So now, as we breathe in, let us fill ourselves with these qualities.(Pause.)

Feel yourself to be completely at peace with all beings... feel the harmony with the earth and every living thing. Know that you are a unique human being with something special to give to the world. Affirm to yourself: I am a being of love and compassion. Breathe in the Universal love and compassion which surrounds you - it is unconditional love, which accepts everything and everyone without judgment, without criticism. So now breathe it into your heart centre and feel it become established there. (Pause.)

You begin to feel a wonderful lightness enter your body... You are becoming so light that you start to rise up... rise up out of your body, into the clear air. Looking down you see the tops of the trees looking like dark green wool, the tops of the trees, and here and there a shining river, winding its way through the countryside. As you rise still further you see towns and cities like on a map, becoming smaller...

You are travelling fast now. You see the outline of the United Kingdom and Ireland... then Europe... becoming smaller... the Atlantic Ocean and other seas... the curvature of the Earth... and then the whole Earth itself, like a large and beautiful blue and green ball. As it becomes smaller it seems to hang in space and you marvel as to how it is suspended there... but you know that it is in its rightful place in the Universe. (Pause.)

We have the thought that this beautiful, incredible Earth is a living , vital organism and as we look at it with love it looks like our home.

We feel sad when we think of all the damage and devastation caused by man to this beautiful planet through his ignorance and lack of care, and through not living in harmony with her as nature intended. But we know we can help in the healing process by thinking creatively and positively, and radiating love and light, as well as in practical ways. We feel a deep sense of gratitude to Mother Earth for sustaining us with her abundant gifts, so now let us send her love and light. We send out the light from our heart centres, visualising her to be whole and beautiful once more, with lush vegetation, clean rivers and seas and pure air, and fruitful and fertile land. (Pause.)

We send out light to the people of the Earth so they may live in harmony with one another and with the planet, living self-sustainably so we may no longer destroy, but are filled with awareness, love and peace. We send out the love and light to all who suffer for any reason, victims of war and natural disasters such as earthquakes and floods, those who have lost their homes or who haven't enough to eat; people who suffer mentally, physically or in any other way. And we also send the light of awareness to those who inflict suffering, either wilfully or accidentally,so that their hearts may be filled with compassion.(Pause.)

Now we send out healing light to anyone known to us personally who may need it - maybe someone you know who is ill, or someone you have a problem with... we send them heartfelt thanks for the lessons they teach us... and make peace with them in our hearts...

Now let us send light to all the animal kingdom... to the birds... the fish... reptiles... insects and of course the mammals... let us send it especially to animals that are suffering right now for any reason, such as ones used in laboratory experiments, or ones who are kept in confined spaces. Let us imagine them roaming once more in peace and freedom. (Pause.)

Now let us send it to the plant kingdom... the trees which provide us with oxygen and also fruit... the food crops... let us thank them for providing us with sustenance... the herbs which are sent for our healing... and for the lovely flowers which give us such joy... (Pause.)

Next we send it to the mineral kingdom... the rocks, the stones and crystals of the earth, and thank them for supplying essential minerals for our bodies. (Pause.)

We feel very much at peace with the earth and all her living creatures, our brothers and sisters. Let us remember that peace begins with individuals... if we can all live peacefully with our neighbours there will be no conflict in the world and peace will reign. (Meditate in silence for a while.)

Now it is time to return to this room... so now imagine yourself returning from the place where you were in space... zooming in, nearer and nearer... you see the earth getting larger... the outline of the U.K.... the cities and towns... coming in ever closer... to this city of Sheffield... to the area above this house... and finally return to your body.

Gradually become aware of your body, how you are sitting, your surroundings. Take one or two deep breaths and when you are ready, open your eyes. Thank-you.

 Quotations - pass bowl round. If anyone has something to share with the group perhaps we can have it after the quotations.

Sing songs.

"Science and religion will meet and shake hands. Poetry and philosophy will become friends. This will be the religion of the future, and if we can work it out we may be sure that it will be for all time, for all people."

James Redfield - The Tenth Insight.

Morning Prayer

O great Spirit of the Universe
I surrender Everything to You
    My thoughts
    My words
    My actions.

Let me flow
    In Your Light
    In your Wisdom
    In your Love
        This day.

39

FLOATING IN THE COSMOS

Preparation for visualisation.

Now feel yourself becoming very light - so light that you begin to float out of your body, up, up into the air, towards the ceiling... then you actually find yourself rising up through the ceiling, through the roof of this building, into the space above. You stay there, hovering for a moment and look around you. Looking down you see buildings, the road, traffic, and people walking here and there... you just observe everything in a detached sort of way. Looking upwards you see the sky... just imagine what it looks like at this moment. (Pause.)

Now you begin to float higher, up into the sky. The only sound you can hear is the breeze. It sounds like a great OM, the primordial sound of the creation of the Universe, as it reverberates down through the centuries.

You are floating further away from the earth now... you can see the outline of the British Isles, then Europe, then some of the continents... (Pause.)

You are travelling faster now, floating right into space and as you do, our sun becomes a distant star, just like the other stars you can see... for you are surrounded by stars, twinkling and shining in the dark sky. Just stay with that for a moment and see how it makes you feel. (Pause.)

There is a sort of vast, invisible grid in space, rather like a gigantic fishing net. Our planet Earth is on the grid, together with all the other planets in the Solar System, and they are all connected with one another. Each planet receives energy and sends it to the next planet. So now let us visualise this grid... and if you see any tears or breaks in the structure, in your mind's eye you can mend them... (Pause.)

You are just floating along, feeling very peaceful and relaxed. You suddenly feel a strong sense of unity with everything... you seem to identify with the stars... indeed with the whole of Creation... you are a child of the Universe... (Pause.)

Some of the stars are large and very bright... others are tiny - just pin-pricks, and you know that they are billions of miles away. They seem to be placed at random, but you know that each one has its own appointed place on the grid, held in position by a sort of invisible glue... and we remember that we, too, are in the place it is right for us to be in, so that we can master the challenges of our everyday lives in order to further our development... if we didn't have challenges in our lives we wouldn't be here, because the Earth is a planet of learning. (Pause.)

However insignificant we may feel compared with the Universe, each of us has a part to play... we are part of a greater reality... it is like a vast jig-saw puzzle, which would not be complete without each small piece... every piece is different. There has never been a person exactly the same as you and never will be again... you are unique in time and space. Each person has a special contribution to make to life... (Pause.)

Now we are going to begin the return journey back to the earth, so we begin to move - at first slowly, then speeding up faster and faster, until we see our planet, many thousands of miles away, but becoming larger as we zoom in. Now we see her suspended in space, a beautiful blue and green planet, hanging there in her rightful place. We have a strong sense that this is our home. Now we are going to radiate feelings of love and peace to the earth, which she needs so desperately, so with all your power focus on sending this out to our Mother, the Earth... (Pause.)

Then we send love and light to all the inhabitants of the earth - to every person, especially to those who especially need it just now - maybe hungry people, or victims of war or natural disasters. Then to the animals... the fish and other sea creatures... the birds... reptiles... insects - all the animal kingdom. Then we send it to the plants... the trees... then the mineral kingdom... all the rocks and stones. Let us visualise the earth whole again, with everyone living in harmony with one another, and at peace. (Pause.)

Now as we approach the earth we can see the outline of Africa... then Europe and Great Britain... then we focus on England ... (approach whichever part is appropriate.) We see the roofs of the houses and the gardens. So we finally return through the roof of this house... through the ceiling, descending into our own bodies once more, with a little jolt... (Pause.)

Become aware of this room, of your contact with the chair you are sitting on (or the floor you are lying on). Notice the sounds in the room... take one or two deep breaths...

You may like to wiggle your fingers and toes, then have a good stretch....
Thank you.

"I am the Sun which is hidden by the shadow of yourself. Cease thinking that you are your shadow and you will find that the sun which I am is your own Reality.

All that frightens and confuses you and grips you is your own shadow. When the Sun of Love manifests in its glory and all faces are turned towards that Radiance, all shadows will have disappeared - even the memory of them will have vanished."

Meher Baba.

Oblation

As I watch the moon behind the trees
I see the Earth turn on its axis.
I am holding it here, in my hands,
Moving, moving oh so slowly,
Cradling, rocking it in my arms -
This precious, precious home of ours.
Now, turning, turning, tracing a sphere,
Then, lifting it upwards
I offer it to the starry sky.

43

A VISIT FROM YOUR GUIDE

Preparation for visualisation.

Imagine that you are somewhere in the mountains... it is winter and there is snow and ice all around. You are standing on a flattish area, a sort of shallow basin, between three peaks. You look all around you and see that the compacted snow is shining with reflected colours... pink... yellow... blue... green and lilac... You breathe in the beauty of the colours... of your surroundings. (Pause.)

Looking around, you notice a waterfall a short distance away. At the top of the waterfall there are icicles, shimmering in the sunlight, and at the base there is a dark pool. You go to look in the pool and see your own reflection... around you is the reflection of the sky, which is dappled with cotton-wool clouds... (Pause.)

After a while you see someone approaching in the distance. The person may be familiar to you, or someone you have not met before. They seem to have a glow about them, like an aura, and you know instinctively that it is someone who cares about you. You look into their eyes and see that they are twinkling with kindness, love and humour... (Pause.)

As this being approaches, you notice that he or she is carrying something... a beautifully crafted box. See the box in your mind's eye... You are presented with this box and you offer your thanks. (Pause.)

You then have the opportunity to ask your Guide a question, so think for a moment what you would like to ask... (Pause.)

The Being looks at you with wisdom and tenderness and if you listen carefully you may hear the answer in your heart. (Pause.)

The message may not come straight away... you may receive it in the near future, even when you are not thinking about it.

The Being stays with you for a few moments, smiling on you benevolently... then gradually fades away... (Pause.)

You open the box and find a gift especially for you, something you feel you need... not necessarily a material gift but a gift of the Spirit... something to further your development, to help you on your journey... (Pause.)

Now it is time to leave this place, so take one or two deep breaths... gradually return to this room...

Afterwards, share your experiences, if wished.

The Guardian Angel.

"Be thou a bright flame before me,
Be thou a guiding star above me,
And be a kindly shepherd behind me
Today, tonight and forever."

Alexander Carmichael.

(Translated from the Gaelic.)

Spirit, Spirit

Spirit, Spirit,
Guide me, guide me
This day.

Spirit, Spirit,
Be with me, Be with me
This day.

Spirit, Spirit,
Heal me, Heal me
This day.

VISUALISATIONS SPECIFICALLY FOR HEALING

MEDITATION ON THE INNER CHILD

Preparation for meditation as before.

Now, in your imagination, I would like you to picture a room. I cannot describe the room, because it is one familiar to you - a room from your childhood, maybe your bedroom.

In your mind's eye, you are sitting in this room; look around you... you recognise some of the furniture... see where the window is and what else is in the room... maybe there are pictures on the walls. (Pause.)
Then, in one corner of the room, you notice a baby's cot. You wonder about this, so you get up and walk over to it. Looking down you see a baby in the cot - a young child. It is you... it is yourself as a child. The child is sleeping peacefully. (Pause.)
Being very careful not to disturb him/her, you reach down and pick up this precious child... you hold him gently in your arms... (Pause.)
You look at the sleeping child and wonder about him... what does life hold in store for this child? What sort of future will he have? (Pause.)

Then you ask yourself, What does the child need? (Pause.)

What can you do to heal this child? (Pause.)

If you could give him something, what would it be? (Pause.)

You may wish something else for the child...(Pause.)

See what answers come into your head. (Pause.)

Maybe these include loving care... unconditional love and understanding... acceptance without judging... recognition of his gifts and acknowledgment of him as a person in his own right, with the freedom to grow and develop as he is meant to do. (Pause.)
You feel a strong bond with the child and that you want to give him some love... so tenderly holding him in your arms you begin to send out some love to him, love and compassion... imagine a bond, a thread from your heart to his heart... gradually the loving feelings penetrate his being, filling him with unconditional love and acceptance... you feel the strength, the power of this love... You accept this child exactly as he is, with all his potential weaknesses and limitations. (Pause.)
When you feel that he is full of your love and compassion, gently lift him up, raise him into the air and bless him, then holding him close, maybe give him a kiss and with great care, you place him back in the cot... then you return to the place in the room where you were sitting. (Pause.)

Gradually return to this room, etc.

"Identify your 'sacred wound' and use it to serve humanity."

Jean Bond - "Behind the Masks."

The Connection

Picking ramsons by the stream,
A peaceful, golden, Spring-like day,
Brought back a memory - a dream?
No, it was real, though far away.

To a meadow, water-edged,
With here and there a shady tree,
My mother took us little girls
To gather watercress for tea.

Crouching by the water's edge
And wondering what we there would find,
We saw the luscious leaves of green
With which the muddy banks were lined.

Taking care so not to fall
And reaching down as best we could,
Our small hands plucked the leafy stems -
Treasure yielded by the mud.

To me it gives unbounded joy -
Consuming food grown in the wild;
It touches something deep inside,
Which can never be defiled.

I know my roots are in the earth,
Connecting me to all that is,
And linking me to folks long gone;
So did my grandmother do this?

Did she on autumn mornings rise
To gather blackberries in the woods,
Fill baskets with sweet fruit and herbs;
In springtime note the opening buds?

51

MAKING THE BODY TRANSPARENT

Relax; deep breathing, etc.

Now I would like you to visualise yourself lying on a beach, maybe in a place which is familiar to you, or in a place of your imagination. Just imagine the beach for a moment - maybe it is sandy, deserted, rocky or whatever... (Pause.)
You hear the sound of the sea ebbing and flowing rhythmically - it does not intrude into your consciousness but you are aware of it like a lullaby. So see yourself lying there, completely relaxed; the sun is shining and you feel warm and comfortable...   (Pause.)

Now in your mind's eye take a look at your skin... at any problems you may have with the skin - any scar tissue or any other marks on your skin... (Pause.)
Now breathe the light of the sun into your skin, and do this until it becomes translucent, transparent... until you can see right through it to the flesh underneath... (Pause.)
Next you are going into your flesh... into the veins, the cells and glands in the flesh, concentrating on any problem areas. Now breathe the light into your flesh until it becomes transparent, and you can see through it to the muscular structure of the body... (Pause.)
Look then at the muscles of your body, not forgetting the tendons and ligaments, concentrating on any weaknesses you may have, or any painful areas... then make them transparent until you can see through them to the organs of the body... (Pause.)
Next, put your attention in the circulatory and respiratory systems including the heart, lungs, and arteries... breathe light into them and make them shine... (Pause.)
Now, concentrate on the other organs of the body... first the sense organs in the head... the eyes... ears... nose... then the organs of the main trunk of your body - the liver... kidneys and then the stomach and the digestive system, not forgetting the colon... include the smaller organs like the appendix and the gall bladder... Next the reproductive organs... just be aware of any problem areas, then breathe light into them, until they become transparent and shining... until you can see right through them to the bones underneath, the skeleton of the body... (Pause.)
So then you go into the bones of your body... first go into the joints, filling them with the beautiful light of the sun, breathing it in and concentrating on any painful areas which you may have... (Pause.)
Then go into the bones themselves, actually into the bone marrow, filling with light, until all your bones become translucent... do this until you can see that the bones are transparent and shining...
So now you are completely transparent, filled with beautiful shimmering light - you are a being of light... (Pause.)

Now, still keeping the light in your body, start to build yourself up again. First see the bones return, but without any problems you may have had... then the organs appear... the circulatory system, the respiratory and digestive systems... the muscular structure... then the flesh... and finally replace your skin. See all of your body return, but in a perfect state, without any problems at all... (Pause.)

Now we are going to protect ourselves psychically from any intrusive forces which may harm us...

So imagine that you are putting on a black, slinky undergarment, like a wetsuit. You draw it up over the feet, up the legs, over the body, the arms and the head, covering yourself completely but allowing you to breathe...

Next you put on a golden suit of armour, made of tiny, brilliant, golden stars...

Finally you put on a cloak, a cloak in the colour and pattern of your choice - the first colour that comes to mind...

See yourself once more lying on your beach, then let the picture fade and gradually return to this room.

Take a few deep breaths, wiggle your fingers and toes; open your eyes.

"There is no need to run outside for better seeing,
nor to peer from a window.
Rather abide at the core of your being,
For the more you leave it, the less you learn."

Lao Tzu.

Earthly Mother Song

From the fruits of all the earth
And the crops which farmers thresh
Comes nourishment which makes our flesh
 Thank you, Earthly Mother.

From the rivers and the lakes,
From the streams filled by the rains
Flows the life-blood in our veins.
 Thank you Earthly Mother.

In the depths of Mother Earth
In the ageless rocks and stones
Are elements which form our bones.
 Thank you Earthly Mother.

We hear the glory of her sounds,
Our marvelling eyes behold her dress
Her wonders make our hearts to bless
 And thank our Earthly Mother.

CLEANSING AND REBIRTH

Preparation for visualisation.

Imagine that you are walking along a path in some woods, wearing the clothes you are wearing now, but also wearing a cloak, the colour of your choice. It will be the first colour that comes into your head. Think also of a taste, and a smell or scent... whatever comes to mind... (Pause.)

In the distance you see some smoke... then, in a clearing in the woods, you see that the smoke comes from a bonfire, which you approach. The fire has cleansing and purifying qualities, and is also empowering. Shiva in the Hindu religion is the destroyer but also the creator; the fire ceremony is one of purification but also of rebirth... so you decide to enter the fire...

As you enter the fire, you shed your outer skin... then your flesh... then the organs of your body... the eyes, ears and other organs in the head, then the other organs of the body down to the bones, the skeleton of your body... At the same time, you shed all attachments, all desires... any negative feelings disappear - you have no fear, no pain, no ambitions, no feelings even - they are all released into the fire... Now your bones become transparent and disintegrate into a little pile of ash. So you feel there is nothing material left of you, only a little pile of dust.... (Pause.)

When the fire dies down, you begin to feel that you will be reborn... a new, whole, healthy, shining person... So you begin to rebuild yourself again, but without the attachments that you had before...

First your skeleton gradually appears... then the organs begin to emerge... the flesh... and finally the skin... and you feel as though you are a completely new person... a shining person... integrated in mind, body and spirit, with the power to be everything you aspire to be... to fulfil your purpose on this planet. (Pause.)

So now you leave this place and as you walk along you meet the divine mothers... There are five of them, and each one gives you a gift... So you take the gifts which have been offered and give thanks... (Pause.)

Finally you protect yourself by throwing a golden cord around your body... this will keep your energy in and protect you from negative influences.

Now, gradually return to this room, making sure that the astral body returns to the physical body. Use hands and feet as magnets if necessary. Open eyes.

Discuss colours, tastes, scents and gifts.

"Dust has no thought of its own - whether it is trampled upon or applied to the forehead of a man, or remains suspended in air or water. It is all the same to it. I tell you, there is no truer and better example of complete surrender than becoming like dust.

Spiritual advancement is a succession of one surrender after another, until the goal of the final surrender of the separate ego-life is achieved. The last surrender is the complete surrender, equivalent to the attainment of Truth."

Meher Baba.

Sonnet

On a disused rubbish tip
Grows a small white flower,
Needing both rain and sunlight
So that it may grow;
Pushing through the rubble
Only seen by sentient eyes.
We need rain and sunlight too,
If a rainbow we would view.

Seen through half-closed eyes
Even tears of pain are sunlit,
Shining with awareness,
Feeling like birth pangs,
Giving rise to
A new understanding.

59

THE CRYSTAL

Preparation for visualisation.

Imagine yourself in a temple. It may be a temple you are familiar with, which you have visited at some time, or it may be one of your imagination. It is peaceful, quiet and beautiful. In the distance you can hear the faint sound of monks chanting in harmony and you can smell a beautiful aroma of incense. (Pause.)

In front of you is a crystal - a clear quartz. It is higher than you and wider... it has a faceted surface so the light is diffused in all directions... and as you look at it, a section of the crystal moves, forming an entrance space... you enter inside the crystal, then the section closes again... (Pause.)

And so you are inside the crystal. All around you is an amazing light which fills you with wonder... After a few moments you stretch out a hand and touch the wall of the crystal. Immediately you are aware of a strong vibration... it is the healing power of the crystal. You sense this immense power, which begins to travel through your fingers, your hand and up your arm... it then disperses and goes to anywhere in the body it is needed... It has the power to heal on all levels - mentally, emotionally and spiritually, as well as helping with physical problems... (Pause.)

So, as you breathe in, allow the power of the crystal to do its healing work... Each time you inhale, breathe in the beautiful light and energy which is enveloping you... (Pause.)

As the power of the crystal takes effect in your body, you begin to feel more in harmony with yourself, balanced and clear minded, with a sense of deep peace... You feel a unity with all living creatures, with the whole of life... (Pause.)

Now it is time to leave the crystal, so gently release your hand from the wall you are touching... the crystal doorway appears once again and you make your exit, noticing that the doorway closes behind you. Once more you are in the beautiful temple... but feeling somewhat different from before... (Pause.)

You know you can return to this place any time you wish.

This visualisation can be used to help heal another person. When inside the crystal, invite the other person to come in with you and see them enter. Then, when touching the crystal, also make contact with the other person by lightly touching their solar plexus centre. Then visualise the power travelling up your right arm, into your solar plexus, down your left arm, through your hand and into their solar plexus. You are a bridge for the healing energy. (Pause.)

You will know when the healing is complete, or the other person will leave when they are ready. So you release your contact from the other person and remove your hand from the crystal wall. The person may wish to say something before they leave. Then say goodbye and watch them leave the crystal.

When you are alone in the crystal, fill yourself with its beautiful light, which cleanses and revitalises you. Take as much as you need of this healing light and feel yourself rejuvenated. Then leave as before.

"To reflect God in all that is
both now and here
My heart must be a mirror
Empty, bright and clear."

Angelus Silesius.

Whinfell Quarry Gardens

The gap in the wall to the old quarry beckons;
As I enter the fern-fringed walkway
The coolness strikes my face
Like a damp flannel.
Lush green plants almost shaking hands
Across the narrow leaf-mould path;
Others, bursting out of crevices
In the ancient, rocky walls.

The increasing peace and stillness
As the road recedes into the distance
Creeps stealthily into my soul,
Heightening my senses
To see, hear, smell, touch the magic.
The raucous cry of a rook
Breaks the silence, and something
Stirring in the undergrowth.
Small, lilac-faced geraniums
In a froth of leaves,
The hypericums, vying with
Each other for space -
Hydrangeas like saucers
With no-one to see.
And is this beauty
Just for me?

ACCESSING ENERGY FOR HEALING RELATIONSHIPS, ETC.

We are going to make contact with the energy which is all around us... the harmonious life energy which orders and organises all life on this planet... it is a healing, holistic energy which affects all of us. Accessing the life energy puts us back into a state of balance and health, with a feeling of oneness with the Universe...

Be aware of the miracle that is you. How marvellous are our senses... our faculties... how do we manage to see, hear and think? What makes us breathe? Even with modern technology it is impossible to recreate a human being, with all the faculties we have in our small bodies. It would take many rooms full of computers to try to emulate our powers and even this would not compare to one molecule, one spark of life within us. (Pause.)

Now breathe in and be aware that the life energy is all around us... the air is full of energy waves and particles... So let us breathe in this loving, harmonious energy... let it settle in your heart centre, relaxing, healing and filling us with its glorious, infinite power, its wisdom and compassion, its peace and serenity... Each time you breathe in, feel the energy in your heart and solar plexus centres, spreading throughout your body. As you breathe out, let it settle and become established... (Pause.)

Now you may think of someone special that you wish to send this healing energy to... name them silently and hold them in your heart... you might like to imagine them surrounded by light... (Pause.)

You may be having a problem with someone, maybe someone at work, or a member of your family. This little exercise will help to improve the situation. So now hold out your arms and imagine that you are holding the person... bearing them on your arms. Now surround them with an aura of golden light... they become lighter in weight and you can raise them upwards... Then radiate the energy to the person, the light of love and compassion. See them full of light until it spreads out into their aura, so they are bathed in light - glowing, shining, smiling and radiant in the light. (Pause.)

Now begin to lower them gently... embrace that person and ask their forgiveness... maybe feel forgiveness in your heart for anything they have done which has harmed you in any way... then gradually let them fade away... (Pause.)

If you have a problem in your personal life... remember that there is always a lesson wrapped up in it somewhere... a precious gift just for you... something you may have been born to learn. If life went smoothly we would not learn anything... so each challenge presents an opportunity for growth... (Pause.)

Try to maintain the feeling of loving energy in your heart, mind and body... the feeling of Unity with all life, with all of creation ...

Now gradually return to this room...
Finish with grounding.

"We shall do well to remember how much we ourselves need forgiveness, and to learn to give freely, judging no man. We know not any soul; but it is our duty, our surpassing joy, to search ever for the spark of the divine in all men."

White Eagle - from "The Quiet Mind."

Rebuilding

Let us rebuild our cabin of Life!
Using the mortar of Self-esteem
We will cement the bricks of Service
Based on the foundation of Love.

In the glass I see *your* face
I can respect your needs
Because I honour my own -
Together we can rebuild the world.

SITTING BY THE SEA

Preparation for visualisation.

Now I should like you to imagine you are by the sea, sitting comfortably on some rocks on the beach, facing the sea which is a little way off. You can see the waves ebbing and flowing, in and out, and you notice the white spray from the water. The sun is shining and the air is clear and fresh.

As you watch the waves, you synchronise your breathing with the movement of the water, so that as a wave comes in, you breathe in gently... exhale as the water ebbs away... (Pause.)

You can feel the warmth of the sun, which begins to fill your whole body, starting with the head... So it comes down into the head, through the violet energy centre, the crown chakra, where it settles as a small sun, then to the deep blue of the third eye... the aqua blue of the throat centre... then it divides and goes down each arm to the palms of the hands, where there are small chakras. In your awareness you feel this energy as a little sun in each palm. It then goes from the throat chakra down to the spring green of the heart centre... and imagine there is a sun in your heart centre... it then continues down to the solar plexus which is a lovely daffodil yellow... then through the lower chakras, the orange sacral centre and the red of the base chakra. At the base chakra the energy splits, going down each leg, through the knees, the lower legs, ankles and into the feet, and once more imagine a small sun in the centre of each foot... So you have small suns in your head, heart, hands and feet... (Pause.)

Now expand the light from each of the suns to spread throughout your body, from the head, heart, hands and feet... to fill your whole body with radiant light. Each time you breathe in, bring in more light, more power... (Pause.)

As it comes into the body it brings the element of fire and the power of the Father energy... which has certain qualities we can bring to ourselves... so as you breathe in, fill yourself with these qualities ...

UNCONDITIONAL LOVE AND COMPASSION ... WISDOM... POWER...
PEACE... TRUTH... COURAGE.... INSPIRATION... (Pause between each one.)

Your feet are planted firmly on the sandy beach.

In the centre of the earth is the Mother energy with its unique properties... now we will bring these into our bodies... So put your awareness into the feet... imagine they have roots which go deep into the earth... we are going to bring the earth energy up through the lower chakras... so as I say each one, breathe it in and feel it settle in your heart... (Pause.)

COURAGE... DEPENDABILITY... PATIENCE... PRACTICALITY... REASON...
STABILITY... STRENGTH... (Pause between each one.)

Now put your attention into your breathing. The air is fresh and cool... as you breathe it in it brings with it the lovely light air qualities. So once more, as I say them, on each inhalation allow them to enter your body...

LIGHTNESS... SPONTANEITY... CREATIVITY... COMMUNICATION... HUMOUR... CLARITY... JOY... (Pause between each.)

You can see the sun reflected in the water, which is constantly moving, rippling, surging and foaming, never still, always changing... The water element gives us the power to be reflective, receptive and intuitive.

So finally we are going to access the properties of the water element... once more take these into yourself as I say each one...

INTUITION... NURTURING ... VULNERABILITY... FLEXIBILITY... RECEPTIVITY... YIELDING... FLOWING... (Pauses between.)

Now move your awareness into the heart centre... there is the father light and power from above and the Mother energy from below... let us now intensify that light, that energy which is really love, unconditional love and compassion...

So now expand and extend that light all around you, so you are sitting in a pool of light and love... (Pause.)

We are all in this pool, everyone in the room... it is a lovely haze of pure white light and love...

Now if you know someone who needs help, or who is suffering in any way, try to imagine them standing in the pool of light... (Pause.) You might like to put in family and friends, or someone you have a problem with, remembering that the people we have difficulties with are our greatest teachers... (Pause.)

Now let us put into the pool anyone on the planet who is suffering - people who are lonely, or who have been bereaved... old people... the hungry... homeless people... anyone suffering from disasters, either natural, like earthquakes, or man-made, like wars... anyone at all who needs light...

Let us now focus on anyone who is harming the planet, either wilfully or in ignorance, and imagine a raising of consciousness among humanity, as the planet will not be healed until there is sufficient awareness of our responsibility as stewards in caring for it... and when we reach a sufficient number of aware people, a critical mass, our planet will reach a point of transformation... (Pause.)

Let us now send it to the animal kingdom... all the creatures on earth, especially ones who suffer at the hands of Man, such as battery hens or ones kept in confined spaces... (Pause.)

Then we put all plants into the light... the trees which are so necessary for our survival... food plants... crops and herbs... fruit trees and all the plants of the earth... and let us thank our mother earth for nurturing and sustaining us... (Pause.)

Finally you might like to imagine that you are enclosing the whole planet in your arms, remembering that we are all interconnected and co-dependent. Imagine that you are gently and tenderly lifting the planet upwards, supporting it with your hands... raising it up... and surrendering it to the Universe, to be in a state of balance and harmony with all the other planets... See it perfect in the light, in its rightful place in the Universe... (Pause.) Each planet sounds its own note and together they make a wonderful harmonic sound. (Pause.)

Now from the place where you are sitting on the beach, gently and gradually return to this room; be aware of the position you are sitting in, etc.

"Man cannot discover new oceans
Until he has the courage
To lose sight of the shore."

Author unknown.

A Meditation

Loving Spirit, we give thanks
For all created things;
Nature's mystic harmony
The healing grace it brings.
We can barely comprehend
Your shining glorious power;
May our consciousness of You
Fill every waking hour.

Wondrous Spirit, Lord Divine
Please use me for your peace.
All bad feelings, thoughts and words
I hereby do release.
Let my faith in You be strong,
And let Thy Will be done.
Lord, You live within my heart
And you and I are One.

VISUALISATION FOR RELEASING NEGATIVITY

Preparation for visualisation.

Imagine yourself walking in a flower meadow. It is a warm day in early summer and the sun is shining... you can hear the sound of birds singing and a river in the distance... (Pause.)

You notice the colours of the flowers - yellow, blue, purple and white... There is a slight breeze blowing and as you walk along you breathe in the clear, pure air... beginning to feel very carefree... (Pause.)

Soon you arrive at the river bank and see the wide, deep river, glinting in the sunshine. It looks very inviting, and as you are feeling very warm you decide to go for a swim, so taking off your outer garments you clamber down the bank and enter the water. At first it feels quite cold and makes you take a sudden inbreath, but soon you get used to it and begin to swim with steady strokes towards the opposite bank... (Pause.)

Now you begin to feel very calm and relaxed... You start to feel that the water is cleansing you, freeing you from all negative emotions, so that any feelings of anger, sadness, fear, resentment, or any other negative feelings begin to melt away... you just let go of any feelings... preconceptions... opinions or judgments... imagine them floating away in the water... Just let go and surrender to the Universe... (Pause.)

You begin to feel very pure and clean inside, empty even, and as you swim, it seems as though you become one with the water... (Pause.)

After a while you reach the opposite bank and start to climb up the slope, noticing the thistles and other plants growing freely there. Reaching the top, you see a grassy patch and lie down to dry off in the sun... (Pause.)

As you are lying there you become aware of your contact with the earth... you breathe deeply and imagine that the breath goes down into your spine, down through the legs and into the earth... try to sense that the earth is breathing as well. You start to experience the Earth as a living being, with an energy circulation of its own... (Pause.)

As you breathe in, imagine that you can sense and feel the circulation of the earth energy flowing through it, and allow it to come into your body... allow the earth's energy to flow into your body and mind... you feel a sense of oneness with the healing power of the Earth... (Pause.)

You sense the strength and stability of the Earth, and as you breathe in, you take in these powerful qualities... strength and stability... bring them into yourself and feel them settle as part of your being... (Pause.)

Relax and breathe even more deeply into the heart of the earth, imagining it as a real beating heart... feel that your heart is beating in time with the Earth's heart... don't suppress any thoughts or try to force them away... simply allow the breath and heart of the earth to be with you... (Pause.) As much as you are able, feel a sense of oneness with the healing power of the Earth... (Pause.)

Now you begin to feel a unity with all of life, with all living things.. a beautiful harmony and peace... (Pause.)

Now gradually return to this room.... become aware of the position you are lying in, and of the other people in the room...wiggle toes, etc.

Finish with a grounding exercise.

"The same stream of life that runs through my veins night and day runs through the world and dances in rhythmic measures.
It is the same life that shoots in joy through the dust of the earth in numberless blades of grass and breaks into tumultuous waves of leaves and flowers.
It is the same life that is rocked in the ocean-cradle of birth and of death, in ebb and flow.
I feel my limbs are made glorious by the touch of this world of life. And my pride is from the life-throb of ages dancing in my blood this moment."

Rabindranath Tagore - from "Gitanjali."

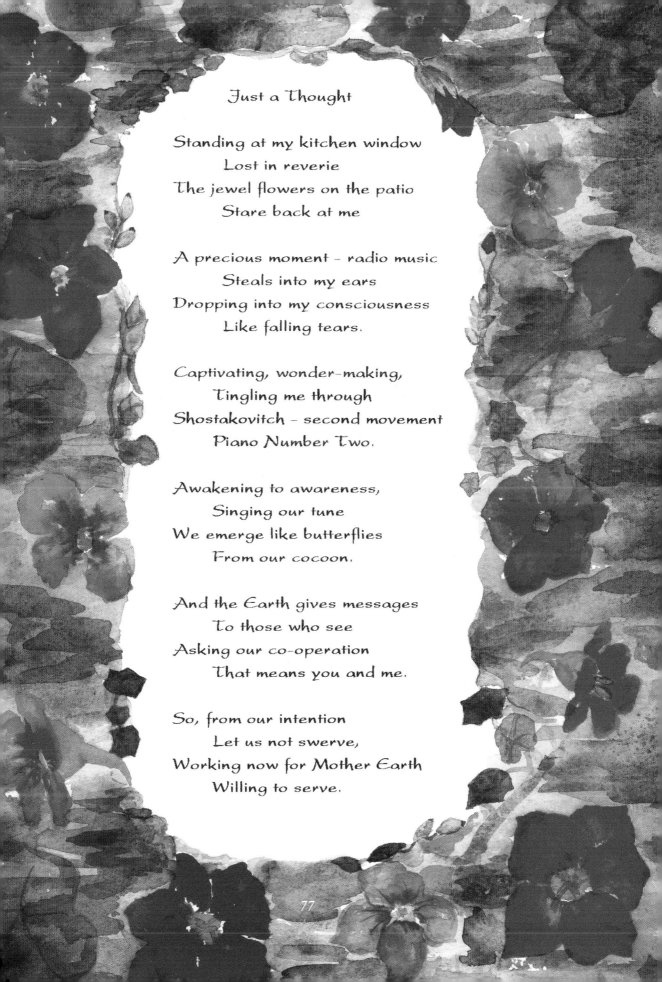

Just a Thought

Standing at my kitchen window
Lost in reverie
The jewel flowers on the patio
Stare back at me

A precious moment – radio music
Steals into my ears
Dropping into my consciousness
Like falling tears.

Captivating, wonder-making,
Tingling me through
Shostakovitch – second movement
Piano Number Two.

Awakening to awareness,
Singing our tune
We emerge like butterflies
From our cocoon.

And the Earth gives messages
To those who see
Asking our co-operation
That means you and me.

So, from our intention
Let us not swerve,
Working now for Mother Earth
Willing to serve.

FLOATING DOWN THE RIVER

Preparation for visualisation.

Imagine that you are up on a mountainside, lying on some grass, very relaxed... there is a stream nearby and you can hear the gentle gurgling of the water... the air is fresh and you breathe deeply into it. (Pause.)

The sun is shining in a clear sky and you begin to feel very warm... the water looks inviting, so you decide to roll over into the stream... and as you do, you feel the refreshing coolness of the water, permeating your whole body... you find yourself becoming very light, then you gradually begin to move with the water, gently floating on the surface, completely relaxed... letting it take you downstream... (Pause.)

After a while you start to notice the landscape on either side of you... the ground is gently sloping, and you can see the purple heather, with here and there some bramble bushes... you can smell the scent of the wild flowers... you look at the water and see it sparkling in the sunshine.

As you lie there you look up at the sky... the sun is still shining, but there are clouds coming across, heavy dark clouds and soon it begins to rain, each raindrop like a tiny cold dart, stinging your body... but then you start to find that the rain seems to be cleansing you, washing away all fear, tension, resentment or any other negative feelings you may be holding in the body... So after a while you feel really clean and empty, quite at peace with yourself... (Pause.)

Soon it stops raining, the sun comes out and you begin to feel warm and comfortable once more... (Pause.)

So you float on and soon you come to a wooded area. As you approach the trees, you feel a little afraid, as they look so tall and powerful... you feel they may overwhelm you. As you enter the wood, the atmosphere becomes dark... you look up to the trees towering above you, but after a while you realise they are not really threatening you, in fact you start to feel that they are quite friendly... and you begin to appreciate their power and beauty... you sense their strength and solidity, which seem to give you energy and power... so you just continue to float on, feeling very tranquil... (Pause.)

After a while the trees thin out and you emerge from the wood... the river has become wide and deep now. Looking downstream you see that there is some turbulence in the water... there are boulders here and there... some of them are quite large, causing you to feel somewhat apprehensive... you think you may be dashed against them. But as you approach each one, you find that the current of water simply carries you around it and you have no need to fear. After some moments you realise that this happens every time you reach a boulder, so you actually have no need to fear at all... you are able to relax and allow yourself to go with the flow of the water... (Pause.)

The river has become very wide now and you see that the land has flattened out... you can see flat plains on either side, with cattle grazing. Here and there are some people working in the fields - they pause to wave to you as you float gently by... it all looks very peaceful in the sunshine. Now you are approaching a village and you notice some small cottages, a church and a school... there are some children playing in the school yard and they stop to wave to you as you pass by, and you wave to them in return...

The river is extremely wide and slow-moving now. Looking downriver you see that it divides into two channels which flow into the sea, making a delta. You have the choice of which channel to float down, but you do not mind which one it is, as you know that each one has something different to show you and to broaden your experience... they both take you to the sea... so you just let the water carry you into one of the channels, and you eventually reach the sea... (Pause.)

You float out into the sea... the waves look rather large and menacing, so you are a little fearful as you approach them... however, you find that as you reach each wave you are lifted up onto the crest of each one... so you begin to enjoy the exhilarating feeling of buoyancy... (Pause.)

You then float further out to sea where the water is calm... you feel you are at one with the water - a part of it... you feel at one with the sea... with the sky... and with the whole Earth... You feel completely at peace... with a sense of the harmony of all things... a unity with all that is... (Pause.)

All around you, the sunshine is causing the droplets of water to evaporate... to be drawn up into the air as water vapour. After a while, you too, begin to feel yourself evaporating... feeling so light, so light that you are drawn up, up into the air... Looking upwards you see a rainbow, a wonderful rainbow with its beautiful spectrum of colours... gradually you are drawn right up into this rainbow, into the colour of your choice... (Pause.)

So there you are shining, shining in the beautiful rainbow. You feel full of joy and peace, completely at one with the universe... (Pause.)

Now, keeping the feeling of peace and lightness, gradually become aware of your body, etc.

"Fear seems to be the greatest enemy of mankind, and the first thing man must strive for is to overcome his fear. Let love rule. There is nothing to fear except fear. Fear is man's enemy and the last to be overthrown. Have no fear. Resign all to the wisdom and the love embodied in Divine law."

White Eagle, from published teachings.

After the storm

After the storm,
The mud;
The river–
A deluge,
Like tears
To wash away
The dirt
The grief
The fear
The anger
And expectations

Making us
Clean
Clear
Whole again.

HIBERNATION - VISUALISATION TO EMPATHISE WITH ANIMALS AND FEEL CONNECTEDNESS WITH OTHERS AND WITH THE EARTH

Preparation for visualisation as before.

You are feeling very warm and drowsy... in your imagination look down at yourself and see a furry body... you are a small furry animal and have just woken up out of hibernation...

You stretch your limbs, take a few deep breaths and look around you. Everything looks dark because you are in a hole in a riverbank, but you can see a glint of light from the opening to the hole... you are in a cosy nest and there may be others with you, of your kind...

You smell the damp, homely scent of the earth all around your nest and you can feel the warm, furry bodies of your family close by. You have a strong sense of contentment and connectedness, a sense that this is your home, and these creatures are your loved ones...

The others are still sleeping. As you are feeling rather too warm you begin to make your way out of the nest, towards the chink of light in the distance, at the entrance to the hole...

When you reach the opening to the outside, the light blinds you a little - it is so bright... but soon you accustom yourself to it and start taking in the beautiful fresh air... you breathe it in... filling your lungs with its coolness and purity. You then become aware of the sound of the birds, chirruping to one another... and you can smell the sweet scent of the countryside plants... (Pause.)

You begin to look around... above is the clear blue sky. To each side is the riverbank, with grass, thistles and small, wild flowers in bright colours. Beneath you is the river itself, sparkling in the sunshine. It is flowing gently and calmly, looking very inviting, so without another thought you plunge straight in...

Being submerged in the cool water is at first a shock to your warm, drowsy body, but it has the effect of awakening you... you suddenly feel very alive and invigorated. After a few seconds you begin to swim across the river, making for the bank opposite. Your head is just above the surface, and as you swim, you become energised and very alert. Everything looks brighter and clearer and you have a sense of being in harmony with the water... as though you are meant to be there... this sense of unity makes you feel very relaxed... (Pause.)

When you reach the opposite bank you leave the water and begin to make your way up the bank, a short distance to the top. There you find some soft grass and as you are now feeling extremely hungry, you start to nibble the delicious, tender, green grass shoots... (Pause.)

As you eat, you feel the warmth of the spring sunshine pervading your body... you feel that you are part of everything around you... the plants which are your food, the breeze ruffling your body, the tall trees around and the clear sky above... you have a sense of oneness with the whole of creation...(Pause.)

Now slowly return to this room and come back into your human body... become aware of the position you are sitting/lying in...take a few deep breaths... roll over and when you are ready, sit up and open your eyes.

"If we can love all life then we see that the butterfly has as much right to live and survive as we do... It is our task in life to make this planet a beautiful place to be, that is why we are here. I know we can do it. I know we will."

Helen Caldicott, M.D.

Bardsey Song

In this place
God is here,
I feel it in my Being.

In this space,
I am here,
Breathing, hearing , seeing.

We are one with God;
You and I are one.

PART SONG

VISUALISATION FOR HERITAGE AND UNITY

This visualisation is about connecting with the earth, re-connecting with our roots and bringing energy to the planet.

In the Universe, the stars and planets are part of a giant interconnecting grid, or web, if you like, which links every planet and star. It is believed by some psychic people that each planet receives energy from the next one and sends it along the grid to the next, and the stars do the same.

On the earth we have energy lines, commonly called ley lines, which have been formed over thousands of years by people and animals walking along the ancient pathways. On these energy lines there are often sacred sites such as churches or stone circles. People who walked these ways felt the power of the energy and were "re-charged" with the life force.

Many of the energy lines of the earth nowadays have blockages on them, caused by man-made constructions such as concrete buildings, roads, telegraph wires, pylons and so on. These have caused blocks in the Earth's energy channels and chakras. In addition to this, the earth's energy system can be blocked by negative forces over the years, such as people's thoughts - dark thoughts of hatred, fear, anger, perhaps sadness or resentment. The spirit realms are trying to unblock and restore the energy flow before it is too late. We can help with this even without visiting any site. One way is to walk the ancient pathways to keep them open, even in our imagination. This work is especially powerful when done by a group.

Thought is a powerful form of energy and by our thought we can help to restore the energy lines and help to heal the planet, by sending out light and positive thought forms like prayers and visualisations.

So now we are going to do a visualisation in connection with this, to reconnect with our roots, with the ancient wisdom and also to help the planet in restoring energy channels...

Sit comfortable and relaxed. Be aware of your position... your feet should be resting gently on the floor. Feel the touch of the clothes against the skin... notice any sounds in the room... and any distant sounds... pay attention to the breathing. As you exhale, release any tension, any worries... see yourself empty of all judgment, opinions or negativity of any kind... smile to yourself and just breathe deeply and steadily... (Pause.)

Now imagine you are in the countryside, maybe in Derbyshire or somewhere where there are hills. You are standing on a road which is quite steep... and you are facing downwards so you can see the road before you, winding down towards a village. There is some mist in the air so the village looks rather faint in the mist...

But now put your attention in the surrounding area. Across the road is a gate leading to a path which leads along the hilltop.

So now you cross the road, walk along the short path to the gate and go through, closing the gate behind you. You can now see that the path follows the contour of a rocky edge, which overlooks views of the valley below... (Pause.)

You decide to follow this path. On either side there is bracken, with some yellow gorse bushes here and there... you can feel a slight breeze on your face... the air is fresh and pleasant...(Pause.)

The path leads to the edge of a plateau and you follow it as it meanders along the edge.

There are large flat slabs to walk on, with boulders and rocks strewn here and there, and as you walk along you have a wonderful view of the valley in the mist. There is a quality of light behind the mist, as though the sun is trying to break through at any moment... it all looks like a magical place... (Pause.)

You suddenly realise how easily you are moving and how easy it is to walk along this path. Your walk has a rhythm to it, almost like a heartbeat or the beat of a distant drum... then you become aware that other people have trod this path before you. There were many, as the path is an ancient route connecting several hill settlements of former times... (Pause.)

You begin to feel a sense of heritage, as though you are in your rightful place and doing something familiar and natural, walking along as people have walked right down through the ages... (Pause.)

After a while you come to a place where the terrain opens out into a flattish basin. There are some standing stones, with one large one in the centre. It is an ancient stone circle. Around the whole circle is a raised grassy bank... (Pause.)

You stand still a moment to absorb the atmosphere of this place. It is still misty and there is a quality of mysticism and strangeness, but at the same time, a sort of familiarity... it seems as though you can somehow sense the presence of unseen beings. The only sound you can hear is the breeze... but if you listen really hard you can hear an "OM" sound, the primordial sound of the planet, which has reverberated down the centuries ever since time began, or even before time as we know it... (Pause.)

Feeling a little tired, you decide to rest on one of the stones, so choosing one of the large, flat stones you lie down...

As you lie there, quite comfortably on your stone, maybe you begin to have the feeling that you have been here before. You feel a strong sense of connection with the stone, the earth beneath, the planet and indeed the whole Universe... a feeling of unity with all living creatures who share this planet... all other human beings... animals... birds... plants... trees... rocks... everything. And you feel a strong sense of belonging, as if you have found your roots. You feel you are contained within the aura of the planet... (Pause.)

You breathe deeply and begin to feel re-energised just by being in this place, as stone circles are centres of powerful energy. You are receiving energy but at the same time you are giving it back to the planet, just by your presence, thereby helping to heal the darkness and sadness of the earth... (Pause.)

Now you may think of someone or some place where you would like to send healing energy, which is seen in your mind's eye as light - a strong, radiant light. So you may like to imagine that person or place surrounded by the light... just hold them in the light for a few moments. Now you may like to send it to a larger group of people who are suffering - even a whole nation... (Pause.) And now let us send it to all the people who are working to help the planet in whatever capacity... let us radiate some energy to them... (Pause.)

Finally send the healing white light to the whole planet... imagine it hanging in space... a beautiful, shining ball of light, in its rightful place in the universe. See it part of the great web in space... now can you imagine all of our solar system bathed in brilliant white light... (Pause.)

Now every planet sounds its own note, so now imagine you can hear the sound the planets make, as they vibrate with energy... together they make a glorious sound, harmonising like a heavenly choir... just stay with that for a moment... (Pause.)

(Sound the OM if wished.)

It is now time to leave this magical place, so you get up off the stone and begin to walk back to the path, and the way you have come. But you know that you can return to this place whenever you wish...

Eventually you reach the gate to the road and are back at the point you started from.

So now gradually return to this room. Take one or two deep breaths...cover your eyes with your hands, then open your eyes slowly... Thank you.

"A vision without a task is but a dream.
A task without a vision is drudgery.
A vision and a task is the hope of the world."

1730. From a church in Sussex.

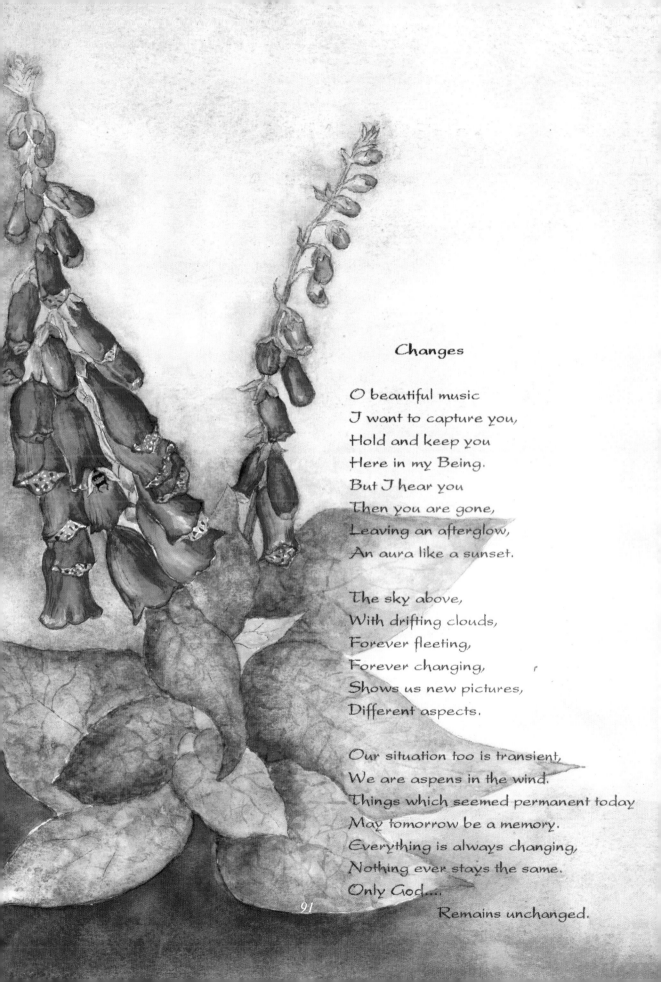

Changes

O beautiful music
I want to capture you,
Hold and keep you
Here in my Being.
But I hear you
Then you are gone,
Leaving an afterglow,
An aura like a sunset.

The sky above,
With drifting clouds,
Forever fleeting,
Forever changing,
Shows us new pictures,
Different aspects.

Our situation too is transient,
We are aspens in the wind.
Things which seemed permanent today
May tomorrow be a memory.
Everything is always changing,
Nothing ever stays the same.
Only God....
                    Remains unchanged.

91

VISUALISATION TO ATTUNE TO THE WHOLE

Preparation for visualisation.

We are going on a journey of exploration.

In your mind's eye, see yourself becoming smaller... you are shrinking, smaller and smaller ... you are now half your size... every bit of you is very small... now you are the size of your thumb, and still shrinking... now you are the size of a pinhead... You are still shrinking, and now you are as big as the point made by a pin. If you could be in two places at once, in your mind's eye see yourself as standing on your own skin, maybe on your leg... look around. (Pause.)

As you look around you, you can see openings here and there... out of each opening comes something spiky, like a tall blade of grass... these are hairs and the openings are hair follicles. You enter one of these and begin to travel down the hair shaft... you can see through the walls of the shaft and here and there you notice some nerve fibres. As you travel along you also see strangely shaped pockets here and there - these are glands and ducts. Also in places you can see a mass of ropes, lying side by side... these are muscles...

You come to the base of the hair duct and enter the tissue beneath. All around you are cells which make up the tissue. You enter one of the cells and immediately become aware of many channels all around you... then you notice you are surrounded by all sorts of objects with strange shapes... some are kidney shaped, some are apple green spheres, some look like bundles of rods... in the centre is a large structure which is the nucleus...and all these objects are made up of atoms... (Pause.)

Now you are becoming even smaller. You are so small that you can enter an atom, which, together with millions of others, make up a cell...

On entering the atom you see another nucleus, as each atom has its own nucleus. Then you become aware of some spherical objects moving round the central nucleus - revolving and swirling. These are electrons, and some of them seem to be a long distance away from where you are in the centre... in fact you are reminded of the solar system with planets travelling round the sun. You can sense a wonderful feeling of peace and harmony, as though everything is doing what it is meant to do... (Pause.)

Everything you see in the atom is held together by a sort of invisible glue. This is Divine Energy, which enables everything to rotate in its place, and organises the atoms of which everything is made. This force of energy holds everything together in harmony... it is a kind of ocean in which everything floats. It is made of positive and negative polarities which balance one another. It fills and organises all life. It is eternal and infinite... the spiritual energy lives forever. (Pause.)

You feel its power and harmony. It is healing energy. Let us now attune ourselves to this healing power... so that it will flow through us... feel the power of this energy pervading your body... (Pause.)

You may wish to put someone into this healing energy... maybe whole groups of people... then animals... plants... all living things... then let us imagine the whole earth basking in this healing energy, in brilliant light... (Pause.)

93

Now let us visualise the whole of our solar system in this light - all the planets in their rightful places, circling the sun, each one following its own orbit, like some vast design... (Pause.)

Now gradually let that picture fade... withdraw from the atom, from the cell, back along the hair follicle... through the pore on the skin... you begin to grow larger... larger... until you are your normal size, sitting in your original place. Take one or two deep breaths, cover your eyes with your hands, and when you are ready, open the eyes.

"Know thyself and thou shalt know the Universe."

Inscribed on the entrance to the Mystery Temple at Delphi.

Who Am I?

I am not anger
I am not pain
I am not greed, nor fear
I am not sadness...

Then who am I?

I am Integration
I am Unity, Harmony
I am boundless Love
Unqualified Compassion....

I am beyond words
I am beyond thought
I am beyond feeling
I am Light ineffable....

I AM.

SHORT VISUALISATIONS TO HELP WITH PROBLEMS

1) If you have a problem, sit in a quiet place, breathe deeply, relaxing as you exhale. As you breathe out, imagine a strong light surrounding you and permeating your body. Lift your arms upwards, open them outwards, then say to yourself, " I surrender it all to God/ the Universe. " Lower arms slowly. Surrender it in true humility and feel the power of your words.

Lift arms again; breathe in; exhale and say, "I open myself to the Spirit of Peace and Tranquillity. "

Saying the words brings the power to you. This is increased with each repetition.
Then feel yourself to be filled with healing power and joy. Keep bringing in the power of the infinite Light and know that nothing can harm you.

This can be done at any time - just breathe in and repeat the phrases you need in the moment.

2) This is about detaching yourself from feelings which may overwhelm you.

If you feel angry, sad, annoyed, rushed, anxious, uncomfortable, depressed, or experiencing any other negative feelings, imagine you are up above the Earth, looking down; you can see yourself ; then watch yourself as an interested but detached observer. This only takes a little practice before you master it. Then, from "above", you observe yourself being angry, irritated, rushing around, etc., in the way that you might watch a drama on television or at the cinema. Continue to watch yourself until you feel more balanced and in control. Then bring in Universal and unconditional Love and Light - breathe it in until you really feel it permeating through your body and spreading out into your aura. (You could say an affirmation here, e.g. "I fill myself with positive energy and am in control of all my feelings.") Ground yourself and return to reality.

This will work on all levels - physical, mental, emotional and spiritual.
As it becomes easier with practice, the feelings affect you less and less. Sometimes you may even smile at yourself as you see how ridiculous it is to rush around, for example, jeopardising your health, in the awareness of a wider context - the vastness and timelessness of the Universe.

I want to make a distinction here between feelings of anger which are justifiable and which you can perhaps do something about, e.g. at animal cruelty, or at some injustice or unfairness when some action may need to be taken, (as not taking action when it is needed is just as soul-destroying as taking some action which may harm someone,) and anger when you are not able to act to address it. Being able to re-act releases the suppressed feelings which cause harm to mind, emotions and even the body.

3) If you feel that something is hindering you, blocking your way and preventing you from moving forward, just sit in a quiet place, close your eyes and slow the breathing down - breathing slowly and steadily.

Now visualise a wall in front of you - a high, wide wall, at a distance of about twenty feet or so. Make it as high as you like, of whatever substance you wish - perhaps it is a solid-looking brick wall, or a massive stone wall...

Now, in your mind's eye, slowly begin to walk towards the wall, keeping your eyes on it. Keep right on going, even though the wall may look insurmountable and impenetrable.

As you approach the wall, something strange begins to happen. The wall starts to look less dense. In fact, as you get nearer it begins to look transparent! And when you get right up to it, you find it is so transparent that you can walk straight through it! So you find yourself on the other side.

A variation of this is to walk up to the wall, press against it and find that a door opens to let you through.

Keeping right on going is the only way to victory!

4) If you have a self-esteem problem, feeling that you are not as worthy or likeable as other people, you might like to try this visualisation.

Imagine you are on a hillside. It is dawn, a few minutes before the sun rises. There is a gentle breeze. You are sitting with your back against a rock, facing the direction where the sun will rise...

The sky is beautiful. Overhead it is quite dark, but in the east the deep blue becomes paler, and there are bands of other colours... green, pink, orange and a beautiful gold... imagine how it is for a moment... (Pause).

As you watch the horizon beyond the distant hills, the sun begins to rise... first you see a point of brilliant golden light on the horizon... as you watch it, it grows larger, lightening the sky all around...

Now as this happens, breathe this beautiful golden light into your body... feel it expanding... as you breathe out, feel it settle into your body. First it goes to the solar plexus, settling there and expanding to the heart centre, then throughout the rest of your body... it takes away any tension, fear, anger, anxiety or any other negative feelings... (Pause.)

The sun is almost completely visible now... as it rises clear of the horizon, take in a deep, deep breath of its pure golden light... it is so bright it is almost dazzling to the eye. The light from the sun is a symbol of love, unconditional, universal love and compassion.

As well as empowering you with love and compassion it fills you with other qualities... truth... peace... and wisdom... (Pause.)

Now take in several more deep breaths. On the first one say to yourself, "I love myself." (Pause.)

On the next breath, say "I love myself as I am now... I am a being worthy of love." (Pause.)

On the next one say, "Because I love myself I can love others... I love all living things." (Pause.)

Now just be with the effects of those words, feeling their power in your body. (Pause.)

You might get into the habit of saying to yourself, e.g. when you look in the mirror, "I love myself. I am a being worthy of love."

5) In a disease such as cancer, where there are unwanted cells in the body, you can imagine that you are in a garden, perhaps a beautiful rose garden, but there are weeds growing between the rose bushes. So you can pull up the weeds one by one and burn them on a bonfire, or see them disintegrate or just float away .

A variation on this is to shoot at little invaders! You can use your imagination to make this as wild and interesting as you wish.

6) To balance yourself and to be more at ease with who you are, imagine a figure eight lying on its side... then put it over your eyes, so that the third eye is at the cross point. Then see a balanced flow of energy moving from one side to the other, travelling up at the centre point, over and down, from one side to the other. This can be used when you feel out of balance.

This technique, from the Book of Earth, was used by our ancestors to balance the left and right sides of the brain, the "masculine" and "feminine".
You can also use it when you want to know something - just picture the figure eight over your eyes and send the energy round, then see yourself at the crosspoint, ask a question, focus, and see what comes into your mind - but you should have no expectations as to the answer!

You may think of other visualisations - be as creative as you like!

"Do you know how important you are? Do you know how wonderful, unique and precious you are? Your essence is as pure and as perfect as an unblemished jewel. You are priceless in your rarity and uniqueness and the universal force values you as highly as everyone else. Now it is time to treasure yourself too."

Caroline Temsi & Caro Handley, "Life Wisdom."